ACCESS THE ACTION!

Scan the QR code to hear this story for **FREE!**

Published in the UK by Sweet Cherry Publishing Limited, 2025
Unit 4u18, The Book Brothers Business Park,
Tolwell Road, Leicester LE4 1BR, United Kingdom

Unit 31, The Pottery, Bakers Point,
Pottery Road, Dún Laoghaire,
Dublin A96 EV18, Ireland

SWEET CHERRY and associated logos are trademarks and/or registered trademarks of Sweet Cherry Publishing Limited.

2 4 6 8 10 9 7 5 3 1

ISBN: 978-1-80263-470-9

Football Rising Stars: Darwin Núñez

© Sweet Cherry Publishing Limited, 2025

Text by Steve George
Illustrations by Sophie Jones

All rights reserved. No part of this publication may be reproduced or utilised in any form or by any means, electronic or mechanical, including photocopying, recording, or using any information storage and retrieval system, without prior permission in writing from the publisher. No part of this publication may be used or reproduced in any manner for the purpose of training artificial intelligence technologies or systems.

The right of Steve George to be identified as the author of this work has been asserted by them in accordance with the Copyright, Designs and Patents Act 1988.

This book is not authorised, licensed or approved by Darwin Núñez Any faults are the publisher's, who will be happy to rectify for future printings.

www.sweetcherrypublishing.com

Printed and bound in India

DARWIN NÚÑEZ

THE UNOFFICIAL STORY

Written by
STEVE GEORGE

Sweet Cherry

CONTENTS

1. A Tale of Two Debuts — 7
2. Resilience and Sacrifice — 15
3. Peñarol — 26
4. Moving to Almería — 36
5. Uruguay's New Star — 45
6. Moving On — 51
7. The Champions League — 61
8. A New Admirer — 70
9. A Season to Remember — 79
10. The Premier League — 88
11. A Work in Progress — 95
12. Liverpool's Number 9 — 101
13. A Qualifying Machine — 112
14. Agent of Chaos — 123

1
A TALE OF TWO DEBUTS

On the 30th of July 2022, Liverpool and Manchester City came head-to-head in the Community Shield – a game between the previous season's Premier League champions and FA Cup winners.

The match was not being played

at Wembley for the first time since 2012, as the famous London stadium was already set to host the final of the Women's Euros the following day. Instead, the two teams would compete for the Community Shield at the home of Leicester City, the King Power Stadium.

All eyes were on the debut of one player in particular ... Erling Haaland. Signed by Manchester City from Borussia Dortmund, the highly-rated Norwegian international striker was already considered

DARWIN NÚÑEZ

 to be one of the best players in the world. He was expected to run rampant in the Premier League.

On Liverpool's bench was also their new big attacking signing of the summer: Darwin Núñez. The Uruguayan forward had arrived from Portuguese side Benfica, where he had scored thirty-two goals in fifty-seven appearances. He was Liverpool's record transfer to date, signing with a total fee of £85 million, bought to replace Sadio Mané after his move to Bayern Munich.

Unlike Haaland, who was starting the match for Manchester City, Darwin would have to wait to show the fans what he could do.

With this match being a close contest between the two favourites for the league title, whoever won would begin the 2022/2023 season with a trophy *and* momentum. There was everything to play for.

Liverpool got off to the best start with a goal from Trent Alexander-Arnold in the 21st minute. Haaland had a couple of chances but missed both and was struggling to get into the game.

★ **DARWIN NÚÑEZ** ★

With the score still at 1-0, Darwin made his debut in the 60th minute, replacing Roberto Firmino. He made an immediate impact, running onto a perfect through ball, but his shot was straight at the Manchester City goalkeeper.

Another new signing making his debut for Manchester City, Julián Álvarez, equalised to make the score 1-1 (the goal being confirmed after a lengthy VAR check).

With the game seemingly heading towards a draw and a deciding penalty shoot-out, Darwin received

★✦ **FOOTBALL RISING STARS** ✦★

a pass and laid it off to Mo Salah before running into the box. Salah's curling cross into the area was met by Darwin, whose header on goal hit the hand of a Manchester City defender. After another lengthy VAR check, it was judged to be handball and a penalty was given to Liverpool. Salah stepped up and scored to make it 2-1.

Into injury time, a Liverpool breakaway saw Salah with another cross into the penalty area. Full-back Andrew Robertson met the ball with a header across goal, where Darwin had drifted between two defenders to find

★ DARWIN NÚÑEZ ★

himself unmarked. He stooped with a low header to put the ball past the advancing goalkeeper, scoring on his debut and sealing Liverpool's victory 3-1.

Darwin ran to the sidelines and loudly celebrated in front of his new fans, getting his first yellow card for removing his shirt.

At the other end, Haaland had one last chance with a saved shot that fell to him just yards out. Even with an open goal in front of him, his shot hit the bar and flew over the top. It was the last action in a disappointing debut for him. It may not have been Haaland's day, but he didn't let that stop him from having many good days throughout the rest of the season.

For Darwin, however, it was a dream start with his new club and another chapter added to a story of success for the young forward.

But this was a story that almost came to a sudden and unfortunate end before it could even begin.

2
RESILIENCE AND SACRIFICE

Darwin Núñez was born on the 24th of June 1999, in the city of Artigas in northern Uruguay.

Artigas sits on the border with Brazil, where the Quaraí River separates

FOOTBALL RISING STARS

the two countries.

A humid, subtropical climate means lots of rain and the threat of monsoons, which causes the river to burst its banks and flood neighbourhoods that sit by it.

Darwin and his family lived in one such neighbourhood in the poorer part of the city. They didn't have much money and struggled to make ends meet, so they often went hungry.

He played football every day with his older brother, Junior, who had taught him everything he knew about

DARWIN NÚÑEZ

the game. It wasn't long before Darwin joined youth clubs, playing for local teams La Luz and San Miguel.

At just fourteen years old, Darwin was spotted by José Perdomo, a former Uruguay international player. Now a scout for Peñarol, his former club, Perdomo recognised Darwin's obvious quality and potential and wanted him to sign for them.

There was just one problem.

Peñarol was based in the Uruguayan capital of Montevideo, nearly 700 kilometres away from

★ FOOTBALL RISING STARS ★

Artigas – a long way for a fourteen-year-old to move from home.

Perdomo went to Darwin's parents and convinced them their son had what it took to become a professional footballer. So, with their blessing, Darwin joined the youth team at Peñarol.

Sadly, it was all too much for Darwin. Alone in a large city far from his home and family, he suffered great homesickness. He couldn't concentrate on football and struggled to adapt. After only a couple of months, he returned home.

DARWIN NÚÑEZ

Reluctant to let the opportunity slip away from him, Darwin wanted to try again the following year. This time, he would have his brother by his side, as Junior had also signed for Peñarol. Their parents agreed to stay with them in Montevideo whenever they could. So, once again, Darwin headed to Montevideo.

Darwin joined up with the Peñarol under 16s team and made up for lost time. Already a fast player, Darwin's physicality improved even more as he grew. This made him very difficult for opposition defenders to deal with.

He based his play off Edinson Cavani, a striker for Paris Saint-Germain at the time, by adopting his style of cutting inside from the wing.

Soon Darwin became unstoppable, expertly dribbling around entire teams and scoring goals from all over the pitch. He was quickly moved to the U23s team and asked to train with the first team.

At only seventeen years old, he was on the brink of playing for Peñarol in the Uruguayan Primera División (the first division in Uruguay)!

DARWIN NÚÑEZ

However, everything came to a crashing halt when he tore the anterior cruciate ligament (ACL) in his knee while playing a game with the U23s side. This is one of the worst injuries a footballer can have – it can change careers or, even worse, end them. Like most bad injuries, it happened from a simple thing: jumping up for a header and landing awkwardly.

Darwin had surgery on his knee, but he remained positive. He felt confident that he would overcome the injury and return to playing.

His difficult childhood had made him resilient, building a strong determination to keep going no matter what.

Recovering from surgery and rehab took time, and then Darwin finally returned to football as promised. But something was wrong. His knee didn't feel right, and there was still an agonising pain that left him in tears after training sessions. Doctors couldn't identify the source of the pain, and Darwin was ready to quit football altogether.

★ DARWIN NÚÑEZ ★

During this time, his brother Junior gave up his dream of playing professional football so that he could return home and provide for their struggling family. He told his younger brother not to quit, believing that Darwin was better suited to making it in football than he was. In an act of brotherly love, Junior had sacrificed his dream so that Darwin could pursue his.

Darwin was inspired by his brother's sacrifice and worked even harder to overcome his problems, helped by his first team coach.

He debuted for the Peñarol first team in November 2017 as a substitute, giving him a taste of what could be.

Shortly after, the pain in his knee was discovered to be bone growth on his kneecap. It would require more surgery to correct, which meant another lengthy spell on the sidelines.

Despite this disappointing news, Darwin wasn't fazed. He'd made it through tough times before, and he was certain this was just another bump in the road to his dream career.

Darwin had learnt at a young age

that nothing was more important than to keep going. In fact, his hardships and recovery journey made him stronger and more determined to be better than ever when he finally returned to playing.

3
PEÑAROL

Almost eight months to the day since his substitute appearance for the first team, Darwin was given his first start for Peñarol in a 1-1 draw.

He made a few more appearances after that, but was used as an impact substitute to run tired defenders

DARWIN NÚÑEZ

ragged and played primarily out on the left wing. Darwin had pace and acceleration, the worst enemy of defenders, and was quickly getting bigger and more physical. However, despite all his good traits, he wasn't scoring goals.

Darwin's first professional goal came in his sixth appearance. In a home game against Fénix, a corner was only half cleared and Peñarol quickly won back possession. After the ball was worked out wide, Darwin

ran into the box between two defenders and met a low cross, slotting the ball past the goalkeeper and into the corner of the net from close range. It was the opening goal of a 2-0 win!

However, it would be his only goal in the 2017/2018 season. He made thirteen appearances in total, starting in six and playing for a full ninety minutes in just one.

Even though he wasn't scoring goals, Darwin was still getting attention for his play and getting noticed for his raw potential – mostly from his national team.

Not long after the season ended, Darwin was called up to the Uruguayan U20s side for the 2019 South American U20 Championships.

Despite going into the tournament as the previous winners and being among the favourites to win it again, Uruguay struggled in the first group stage. A win against Ecuador, a surprise defeat to Peru and a not very surprising defeat to Argentina meant they needed to win against Paraguay in the last game of the round to advance.

Having played in the previous three games, Darwin was on the bench for this important match. Luckily, his team didn't need him. They won 1-0 against Paraguay and made it through to the final group stage.

Uruguay started well with a draw against Venezuela and two wins against Ecuador and Brazil, but they finished the tournament disappointingly with a defeat to Argentina and a 0-0 draw with Colombia.

DARWIN NÚÑEZ

The team ended up finishing third in the tournament. Darwin scored no goals and made one assist in six appearances.

His first international goal came a few months later in a friendly against Senegal U20s. The match was a warm up game for the 2019 FIFA U20 World Cup, which Darwin would also be playing in.

Uruguay's first group game of the U20 World Cup was played against Norway, so it saw Darwin facing off against upcoming star Erling Haaland.

While Haaland did not score, Darwin did! His goal came from a brilliant shot outside the penalty area that looped over the goalkeeper. Uruguay wrapped up the match with two more goals, winning 3-1.

Darwin scored again in the final group game against New Zealand, helping Uruguay top the table and easily make it to the knock-out stages. However, their tournament was over in the next game, with a 3-1 defeat to Ecuador.

DARWIN NÚÑEZ

Although the national call-ups were a great step for his career, it meant that Darwin was missing out on playing for his club. He missed the first half of the season mostly through international duty.

When he finally returned to club duty, he carried over his good form and confidence. He became unstoppable, even scoring a hat-trick for Peñarol against Boston River.

The first goal came after a clearance from a corner was hoofed upfield from inside the penalty box, straight over the midfield and into the opposition's half. Darwin easily outran three defenders, got the ball and sprinted into the penalty area, followed by a nice finish past the goalkeeper into the corner of the net.

The second goal happened after a run from a Peñarol midfielder kept the defence busy, allowing Darwin to drift into unmarked space on the left. The midfielder passed the ball to him, then Darwin hit an amazing first-time side-foot shot to curl the ball around the diving goalkeeper.

The third and final goal was the best of them all. After some nice one-two

DARWIN NÚÑEZ

passing, Darwin ran onto a through ball and burst into space, before hitting a low hard shot from the edge of the penalty area into the goal at the near post.

It was Darwin's first professional hat-trick, and it was also the last time he'd score goals for Peñarol.

Over in Spain, second division side UD Almería found themselves with some money to spend after a takeover. They wanted to make a statement with whoever they signed, and they had their eye on the young Uruguayan who looked to be the next big thing.

4
MOVING TO ALMERÍA

UD Almería is a relatively new football club, formed in 1989 in the south-eastern Spanish city of Almería. The club has spent most of its time in the Spanish second division, first entering La Liga (the Spanish first division) in 2006, under the management of

DARWIN NÚÑEZ

Unai Emery. Almería then bounced between the two leagues for a short while, before getting stuck in the lower half of the second division for a few years.

In 2019, Almería was taken over by a new owner who injected a lot of money into the club. They wanted to return to the first division, so nine players were bought to make it happen. The manager, Pedro Emanuel, already knew exactly who he wanted as his new striker.

 **★ FOOTBALL RISING STARS ★**

Despite attracting attention from other clubs across Europe, Darwin was still relatively unknown. Most of the clubs that were interested in him were waiting to see how his potential would grow before revealing their intentions. However, Almería didn't hesitate and had no worries about making him their biggest signing to date.

Darwin had a tough decision to make. If he thought moving away  from his home was tough, how would he feel after moving overseas, well over 9,000 kilometres away? It helped that Darwin's first language was Spanish (it is spoken throughout Uruguay, a former Spanish colony), and he knew that a move to Spain would advance his career and put him properly in the spotlight.

He agreed to a five-year deal, and Almería paid an initial $4.5 million for him. This was a massive transfer fee for a club in the second division to pay. It was a big gamble for both Darwin and Almería.

Thanks to the move, Darwin was able to provide for his family and repay them for the sacrifices they'd made. He'd always promised to buy them a new house when he signed his first big contract, so that's what he did.

Darwin bought his family a new house with six hectares of land, which is a massive amount of space! Eight full-size football pitches fit onto six hectares of land, with room left over for changing rooms, merchandise stands and a few burger vans. But it didn't matter to the Núñez family how big the house and land was. Most importantly, they were so proud of

★ DARWIN NÚÑEZ ★

Darwin and overjoyed that he was living his dream as a successful footballer!

Darwin was determined to hit the ground running for his new opportunity. He hired his own nutritionist to help with his diet and a personal trainer to help with his fitness, as well as developing his tactical knowledge.

He had to wait to make his debut for his new club, finally coming into a match against Sporting Gijón as a substitute on the 3rd of October 2019. Unfortunately, he was on the losing side. Almería lost 4-2.

★★ **FOOTBALL RISING STARS** ★★

Another short substitute appearance followed, and then he got his first start and first goal for the club.

Almería was playing at home against Extremadura, and Darwin was in the starting lineup. For an hour, the game remained deadlocked at 0-0. Almería had gone six games without a win, and it looked like this may be game number seven.

After a corner was hit into the box, both Darwin and his teammate went

 for the loose ball and were fouled at the same time – an impressive and

★ DARWIN NÚÑEZ ★

unwanted feat for Extremadura, as it cost them a penalty.

Darwin took the ball and placed it on the spot, showing no sign of nerves or pressure in taking a penalty in his first full start, and in front of his new supporters. With the score at 0-0, the pressure was on to score and break Almería's winless streak.

Extremadura's goalkeeper dived the right way, and for a moment he may have thought he would save it. But what he didn't know, not until the ball had already shot past him in a blur, was that Darwin could hit the ball very,

very hard. Even the fans behind the goal didn't realise that the ball had gone in, not until the net sprung back into shape and the ball bounced across the back of the goal. By then, Darwin was already celebrating.

Darwin was substituted off shortly after as a precaution, since he had taken a knock.

Almería scored two more goals, and a late comeback from Extremadura made it 3-2 – but Almería held on to win. Darwin's penalty had opened the game up and helped his team win!

5
URUGUAY'S NEW STAR

October 2019 not only marked Darwin's first club debut and goal for Almería, but also his first appearance and goal for his country's first team.

Selected for the squad in a series of friendlies, he was on the bench for most of them. In a game against Peru, with Uruguay losing 1-0, Darwin came onto the pitch to add his signature pace and power to the attack.

A cross was whipped into the box from the left wing, and both Darwin and a defender dived head first at the near post. Darwin got himself in front of the defender and reached the ball first. What was remarkable about it was the way Darwin managed to slightly shift his body to connect with the ball – to the point where he was actually facing away when he headed it towards the goal.

His shot was still on target, and

although the goalkeeper got a hand to it, he could only push it into the side netting. Darwin's momentum made him slide on his back across the penalty area as he looked and saw the ball go into the goal. He jumped to his feet and slid on his knees towards the corner flag, where his teammates all surrounded him. No more goals were scored, so the friendly ended 1-1.

Back at Almería, Darwin's confidence and form grew even more. Quickly becoming a standout player, his pace scared defences, his power outmuscled them and his technical skills surprised them. He brought everything to the side his manager wanted of him, scoring sixteen goals in thirty appearances to keep Almería in the promotion places throughout the 2019/2020 season.

However, a bad run of results at the end of the season saw them finish fourth – outside of the automatic promotion places. Instead, Almería had to try and progress via the play-offs.

⋆* DARWIN NÚÑEZ *⋆

After losing the first leg of the semi-final 1-0 against Girona, they needed to win the second leg by two goals. Despite Darwin getting an assist, Girona scored twice and won 1-2. This meant that there would be no promotion for the ambitious Almería yet.

Darwin finished the season as one of the league's top goalscorers, and his efforts throughout had yet again alerted other clubs to his talent (the ones that had waited to see how he would develop). Now that they knew what he was capable of, it wouldn't be long until one of those clubs came knocking with an offer.

6
MOVING ON

Around this time, Barcelona heard about a young player from a team in the Spanish second division. The rumour was that Darwin would be huge, so they needed to get him now while they could.

Despite this, Barcelona did not sign Darwin. Maybe they thought

 someone playing in the second division wasn't good enough for Barcelona? Maybe they just didn't want to admit that money was tight and they couldn't afford him? Whatever the reason for Barcelona not taking a risk, they let Darwin Núñez slip through their fingers – a massive mistake.

Instead, one of the best teams in Portugal, Benfica, swooped in to sign Darwin for €24 million – the biggest ever transfer fee for a player from Almería, or any other team in the

✯ **DARWIN NÚÑEZ** ✯

Spanish second division. The deal also included a sell-on clause that guaranteed Almería would receive 20% of any future transfer, which would result in a huge payout for them very soon.

Benfica played in the Primeira Liga (Portugal's top league) and were the most decorated club in Portugal to date. Since their formation in 1904, they had won eighty-six major trophies! The move would be a great chance for Darwin to add some winner's medals to his own honours list.

Darwin's transfer was part of a huge investment in player transfers by the club, mostly funded by a massive €68 million transfer fee received for defender Rúben Dias when he moved to Manchester City.

Darwin made his debut as a substitute in the second half of a 2020/2021 Champions League qualifier, just eleven days after signing for the club. It was not one to remember, as a 2-1 loss ended the campaign before it even began.

Benfica's luck changed when their league campaign got off to the best

DARWIN NÚÑEZ

 possible start with five back-to-back wins. Although Darwin only scored one goal in this run (thanks to a goalkeeper running out of his area and leaving the goal wide open for Darwin to easily score), he also made five assists in his first four games.

In addition to that, Darwin had already made a statement at the club in a different competition. After failing to make the Champions League, Benfica had another chance to play European football in the Europa

League, entering the group stage alongside Lech Poznań, Standard Liège and Rangers.

In the first group game against Lech Poznań, Darwin scored a hat-trick with two headers, a superb spin *and* a first-time shot. Darwin scored two more goals in the group games, and Benfica went on to qualify for the knock-out stage with ease.

However, it was a difficult season overall. The COVID-19  pandemic swept across the world and disrupted everything, so football

DARWIN NÚÑEZ

and other sporting events were temporarily stopped.

Darwin caught the virus and was out for three weeks. This was on top of other injuries he'd also picked up, and he didn't score a goal for a while as a result. Although he'd impressed many in his early games, helped by the hat-trick in the Europa League, he started to fade a little and questions about his worth were starting to be asked.

Benfica didn't win anything in the 2020/2021 season, making them trophyless for the first time since 2012.

They were knocked out of the Europa League by Arsenal in the first knock-out game, and they also lost both domestic cup competitions to SC Braga – including a 2-0 defeat in the final of Portugal's main cup competition, Taça de Portugal. Despite qualifying for next season's Champions League with a third-place league finish, it was considered a disastrous season for the expectant Portuguese side.

Darwin scored fourteen goals and made twelve assists in a total of forty-four appearances in all competitions.

DARWIN NÚÑEZ

It was not the return he and Benfica would have wanted. But as we know, Darwin is very resilient – something he showed once again when he needed more surgery on his knee after the season ended. Having this surgery meant that he missed the chance to play for his country in the 2021 Copa América – North and South America's prestigious version of the World Cup and European Championships.

Thanks to his resilience and desire to return stronger than ever, Darwin recovered from surgery in record time. He was feeling much better about one month ahead of when he should have.

He was determined to make the 2021/2022 season his best one yet. Barcelona was about to hugely regret not signing him, but Liverpool would get a hint of things to come ...

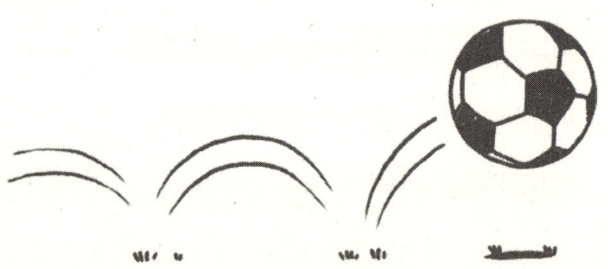

7
THE CHAMPIONS LEAGUE

Benfica qualified for the 2021/2022 Champions League group stage after beating Spartak Moscow and PSV Eindhoven in the qualifying stages. Although Darwin was absent due to recovering from his knee surgery, they easily made it through to the group stage.

Drawn against Dynamo Kyiv, Bayern Munich and Barcelona in Group E, Benfica would have to fight for their place in the knock-out round. It was a difficult group, but it allowed Darwin to show Barcelona what they missed out on by not signing him.

After drawing 0-0 with Dynamo Kyiv in their first group match, Benfica were set to face Barcelona next.

It took only three minutes for Darwin to prove his worth.

★ DARWIN NÚÑEZ ★

From just inside the Benfica half, midfielder Julian Weigl chipped the ball forward between two Barcelona defenders. Darwin sprinted after it, collecting the ball and racing down the left wing. With the ball heading towards the corner, the danger seemed minimal – but Darwin cut inside, running at a defender. After a couple of stepovers, he left the defender scrambling and knocked the ball to the right.

Hitting a low shot just as the ball remained within reach, Darwin managed to get it on target at the

★★ FOOTBALL RISING STARS ★★

 near post, beating the goalkeeper. Benfica were already 1-0 up and the game had barely started!

Darwin was a constant thorn in Barcelona's side, defending from the front, putting pressure on defenders and creating chances.

He almost scored a second goal, too. After the Barcelona keeper came racing out of his area, Darwin easily beat him to the ball and darted around him. It looked like a certain second goal, but he was unlucky and ended up hitting the post from distance.

DARWIN NÚÑEZ

Rafa Silva scored in the 69th minute, putting Benfica ahead 2-0.

A foul in the box gave Benfica a penalty late into the game. Darwin placed the ball on the spot, took a couple of steps back and hit the ball low in the left corner of the goal, sending the goalkeeper the wrong way. The game ended 3-0! It was a great result that put Benfica in a good spot in the group.

However, two heavy defeats against Bayern Munich threatened to derail them. Benfica scored no goals in their home match, losing 0-4. Darwin

★ FOOTBALL RISING STARS ★

scored after coming on as a substitute in the second match, but it wasn't enough. Bayern won 5-2.

Benfica then drew 0-0 with Barcelona, so it was all to play for in the last group game.

With Bayern Munich comfortably leading the group, the battle for second place was between Benfica and Barcelona. Benfica had the easier tie against Kyiv, while Barcelona had to travel to Germany to face Bayern Munich.

Benfica won their match, already ahead 2-0 when Darwin came on

✦★ DARWIN NÚÑEZ ★✦

as a very late substitute in the 82nd minute.

Barcelona lost 3-0 to Bayern, so Benfica qualified for the knock-out stages at their expense.

In the round of 16, they played against Dutch champions Ajax. The first leg took place at Benfica's home of Estádio da Luz, ending in a 2-2 draw.

Having two away goals and playing at their home stadium, the Amsterdam Arena, Ajax should have had the advantage in the second leg.

Despite this, Benfica chose to sit back. They had been playing a counter-attacking game in the Champions League, utilising Darwin's speed to hit teams on the break. Ajax had 61% possession and sixteen shots compared to Benfica's four. It was one of those four, however, that made the difference.

In the 70th minute, Benfica won a free kick deep on the right wing – so deep it was practically a corner. The ball was looped into the penalty area, high and hard to the six-yard box. Darwin easily shrugged off his marker and jumped to meet the ball perfectly,

DARWIN NÚÑEZ

powering a header into the back of the net to make it 1-0. He ran around the goal and celebrated with the travelling Benfica fans.

A few minutes later, he fell to the ground with an injury while running after the ball, which took him out of the game. Luckily, it was just a tweak and nothing serious.

Benfica held on to win, ready to face Liverpool in the next stage of the competition.

8
A NEW ADMIRER

As the second half of the Champions League quarter-final against Benfica began, Liverpool manager Jürgen Klopp stood on the sidelines and watched closely.

Although his side were comfortably in the lead 0-2, Benfica had caused

★ DARWIN NÚÑEZ ★

them some issues. Or to be more precise, *Darwin* had caused them some issues. All Liverpool had to do was see the game out or score another goal to finish the job.

But it wasn't that simple.

Liverpool defender Ibrahima Konaté made a mistake, letting the ball go through his legs on the edge of the six-yard box. An unfortunate event, made more unfortunate by the fact that Darwin was just behind him.

Despite not expecting the ball to reach him, Darwin controlled it well, taking a light touch with his left foot to knock the ball to his right. With a well-placed curling shot, he put the ball into the net to make it 1-2.

Instead of celebrating, Darwin grabbed the ball and ran with it to the centre spot. He'd obviously sensed a momentum shift and was eager to restart the game.

Both teams pushed to get another goal, but it was Liverpool who scored in the 87th minute. An equaliser had been a real possibility, so the Benfica fans' worst nightmare was to concede

★ DARWIN NÚÑEZ ★

so late in the game. Worse still, the goalscorer was Luis Díaz, who used to play for their hated rivals, Porto. It would be a very difficult task to overturn this result at Anfield in the second leg.

Even still, Darwin had impressed them all. He was having an outstanding season in the league and his form had carried over to the Champions League. He went toe-to-toe with an impressive Liverpool defence, outrunning full-backs Andrew Robertson and Trent Alexander-Arnold, and more than holding his own physically against

★ FOOTBALL RISING STARS ★

Ibrahima Konaté and Virgil van Dijk.

In a press conference before the second leg, Klopp was asked what he thought about Darwin. With his famous toothy smile, Klopp praised Darwin's skills and said he should stay healthy to have a good career ahead of him.

Reading between the lines, it is clear that Darwin was firmly on Klopp and Liverpool's radar at this point. The throwaway comment about him staying healthy (meaning injury-free) could've been Klopp's way of showing interest without being too direct or

★ DARWIN NÚÑEZ ★

alerting other clubs to his intentions.

But Liverpool weren't the only club in the Premier League to have noticed Darwin's potential, as he had already attracted the attention of several others.

In the January transfer window, West Ham United's €45 million bid (plus add-ons) for Darwin was rejected by Benfica. Newly cash-rich Newcastle United were also rumoured to have had meetings with Benfica about a big money transfer.

★★ FOOTBALL RISING STARS ★★

As Darwin's fame grew, so did the interest of higher-profile clubs. Manchester United, Paris Saint-Germain and Atlético Madrid were all said to be ready to pounce.

In the second leg of the Champions League quarter-final at Anfield, Benfica's hopes of a comeback were crushed early when Liverpool scored after twenty minutes.

Darwin thought he'd scored the equaliser when he ran onto a through ball and chipped it over Liverpool's goalkeeper, Alisson.

★ DARWIN NÚÑEZ ★

It was a world-class finish ... but the goal was disallowed for offside.

On the sidelines, Klopp had a telling wry smile on his face.

Benfica finally got a goal back, then almost took the lead as Darwin hit a great volley from the edge of the penalty area. It looked like it was definitely going in, until Alisson made a last-ditch diving save.

In the second half, Liverpool scored two more goals. Benfica rallied and scored another goal, before Darwin finally scored himself – beating a defender and poking the ball past the goalkeeper. It ended 3-3, but Liverpool won 6-4 overall.

Benfica's Champions League run had come to an end. Darwin had scored six goals from ten appearances in the tournament, making him Benfica's top-scoring player in the competition in just one season. His success made him a sought-after player and cemented his place amongst the top forwards in Europe.

But it was in the Portuguese league where he was truly made.

9
A SEASON TO REMEMBER

Darwin missed the first two Primeira Liga games of the 2021/2022 season as he recovered from his knee operation. In the third game, he finally came on as a late substitute.

Any doubts about the after-effects of the operation or his knees making it a difficult season for him were quickly squashed, when he scored two goals in a 0-5 thrashing of Santa Clara and then two more against Boavista.

His short run of games without a goal ended when he scored nine goals in just five games, including two hat-tricks, before a foot injury came at the worst time. The injury meant he had to miss the game against fellow title chasers Porto, which Benfica then lost 3-1.

⭐ DARWIN NÚÑEZ ⭐

Darwin quickly returned, scoring another seven goals – including yet another hat-trick – to keep Benfica's title hopes alive.

Darwin ended the season with twenty-six league goals in twenty-eight appearances. He was the league's top goalscorer by six goals, winning him the Bola de Prata trophy as well as Player of the Year.

Despite Darwin's goalscoring, Benfica ended the season trophyless … again. They finished the league in third and were knocked out of the domestic cup in the fifth round.

★ FOOTBALL RISING STARS ★

In all competitions, Darwin scored thirty-four goals and made four assists in forty-one games. He was having an excellent season. It looked like he was playing the league on easy mode, tearing defences apart and scoring goals for fun!

Everyone expected him to move on from Benfica, even though he was only two years into his five-year contract. These expectations were boosted when Darwin publicly announced that he had got a new agent.

⭐ DARWIN NÚÑEZ ⭐

An agent's job is to get their client the best deal (which usually includes more money and transfers to the top teams), and choosing a high-profile agent sends a message that you intend to do something big. By signing with Portuguese agent Jorge Mendes, Darwin had done just that.

Mendes was very experienced, having represented Cristiano Ronaldo, David de Gea and João Félix. He'd also worked with other well-known sportspeople, including Ferrari Formula 1 driver Charles Leclerc.

★ FOOTBALL RISING STARS ★

Darwin had already rejected bids from West Ham and Newcastle, so rumours spread that he wanted to move to a club that had won the Champions League.

With Mendes as his agent, the focus shifted to the likes of Manchester United and Paris Saint-Germain. It certainly didn't look like he would be going to Wolverhampton Wanderers, like many of Mendes's up-and-coming clients do.

Liverpool was also a contender for Darwin. Jürgen Klopp had been keeping an eye on the Uruguayan player for a while now – perhaps

★ DARWIN NÚÑEZ ★

even before the Champions League matches. Either Klopp had made his mind up by then and was going to sign Darwin, or the deal was already done and he had got a pleasant taste of what Darwin was going to bring to his Liverpool side.

With Sadio Mané wanting to leave, Klopp needed a replacement for the left-sided forward. So when Mané went off to Bayern Munich, Liverpool announced who would be replacing him ... Darwin!

Darwin moved to Liverpool for a fee of £64 million, with add-ons that could potentially take the total to £85 million – a club record! And thanks to the sell-on clause, Almería would receive 20% of the total.

At only twenty-two years old, Darwin already had combined transfer fees of over €100 million, having been a record signing for each club he'd joined.

The move to Liverpool put a huge weight of expectation and pressure on Darwin's shoulders, and yet he continued to show resilience and determination to overcome any obstacle.

★ **DARWIN NÚÑEZ** ★

Marking his debut with a goal and standout performance while also overshadowing the other big signing of the summer, Haaland, in the Community Shield opening game put him in a good position for the season ahead.

10
THE PREMIER LEAGUE

Scoring goals is a good way to make an impression and get noticed. Headbutting an opponent, however, is absolutely not. And Darwin happened to do both during his first two Premier League games.

Making his league debut for

★ **DARWIN NÚÑEZ** ★

Liverpool on the opening day of the 2022/2023 season away to Fulham, Darwin came off the bench and immediately changed the game.

Fulham clung onto a 1-0 lead, but Liverpool kept pressing. As Darwin ran onto a short low cross from Mo Salah, beating a defender, it looked like he had overrun it. But in a moment of genius, with the ball behind him, Darwin managed to use the back of his foot to flick it into the net to level the score at 1-1.

★ FOOTBALL RISING STARS ★

A penalty to Fulham made it 2-1, but then Liverpool equalised again after Darwin assisted a goal from Salah. While Darwin may have actually been trying to control a cross he wasn't expecting to reach him, which then happened to fall nicely for Salah, a goal *and* an assist in his first game for Liverpool was still something to be proud of.

It was an almost perfect introduction to the league and gave the Liverpool fans a great first impression of what was to come from Darwin.

★ DARWIN NÚÑEZ ★

The next game was played in front of his new fans at Anfield, the home of Liverpool, and Darwin was in the starting lineup. This should have been the perfect opportunity to prove himself to the home fans, but Darwin made a very different impression … Having had an on-pitch battle that was starting to turn a bit nasty with Crystal Palace defender Joachim Andersen, the two players had yet another heated exchange.

Andersen shoved Darwin in the back, who then reacted unwisely by turning and banging his head

 against Andersen's. Unfortunately for Darwin, Andersen reacted badly and immediately fell to the floor. The rules of the game said it was a violent act, so Darwin was given a red card for the incident. It was the old classic trick of winding up an opponent until they react in the worst way, and Darwin fell for it.

Thankfully, he learnt his lesson and only received two yellow cards in all competitions for the rest of the season – and no further red cards.

DARWIN NÚÑEZ

But it wasn't just yellow cards Darwin was avoiding. Goals were also becoming rare. By the end of 2022, Darwin had scored just seven goals in the Premier League and the Champions League combined. The previous season at Benfica, he'd already scored eighteen goals by the end of the year.

Perhaps the high expectations were getting to Darwin? Being the club's most expensive signing and having a great previous goalscoring record seemed to weigh heavy, and the pressure to perform was affecting his game.

Patience is not practised much, if at all, in the Premier League, but sometimes it takes a little bit of time for things to fall into place.

11
A WORK IN PROGRESS

All players have bad games and dips in form, even those who are considered to be the greatest in the world, and Darwin was no different. No matter how hard he tried, his lack of goals meant that there was always someone judging his every move.

Opposition fans are particularly quick to point out when a player is doing badly. They enjoy every error or missed chance, even if it's just by a centimetre or two, and they love it even more when the mistake is an embarrassing one. Although it's not so funny when a player from *their* team easily loses the ball, or sends it flying over the bar in front of a completely open goal.

Pundits are also one of the loudest critics. Even ex-players turned pundits who have made the same mistakes

DARWIN NÚÑEZ

themselves are quick to point out where a player is going wrong ... before, during and after a game has finished. They were quick to analyse Darwin's dip in form, commenting that perhaps he was struggling to adapt to his new club.

Darwin's shortage of goals wasn't for a lack of trying. By the end of 2022, he'd made fifty-two attempts on goal. But he'd also missed fourteen 'big chances' and hit the post five times.

The fact that Darwin was getting into good positions and creating plenty of chances was being overlooked, but his overall game was receiving praise from some people – most importantly, from his manager. Unfortunately, the majority of fans were still focussing on just his goalscoring record.

However, it only takes a couple of goals, or even just a couple of good performances, for everyone to change their minds about a player.

In February 2023, Darwin and Mo Salah were the most productive pair in the Premier League, creating a chance every fifty-two minutes. Darwin was also named Player of the Month for February.

After goals against Real Madrid and Manchester United, the pundits who'd previously said he was struggling were now saying how well he had settled into Liverpool.

Darwin's first season with Liverpool may not have met expectations, but he had done enough to earn praise and show a glimpse of what he could offer in the future. He scored fifteen goals and made four assists in forty-two games across all competitions.

Ultimately, Liverpool fell short and finished fifth in the league – outside of the Champions League places. It was clear that the side was starting to age and needed an overhaul.

Like the team, Darwin was also still a work in progress.

12
LIVERPOOL'S NUMBER 9

Going into the 2023/2024 season, older players such as James Milner and Jordan Henderson left on free transfers and Liverpool began their overhaul.

The club brought in Alexis Mac Allister, Ryan Gravenberch and

★ FOOTBALL RISING STARS ★

big-money signing Dominik Szoboszlai to put younger, fresher legs in the midfield.

Despite serious interest from Saudi Arabian clubs, Mo Salah decided to stay with Liverpool.

After the departure of Roberto Firmino, Darwin was given the number 9 shirt – a sign of the faith and confidence Klopp had in the young Uruguayan to lead the line.

Darwin was honoured to be given the shirt number and took steps to show he deserved it, scoring two goals in a 1-2 win against Newcastle

★ DARWIN NÚÑEZ ★

after Liverpool had been losing 1-0 and were down to ten men.

Darwin's season only got better, and he was often the first player to reach certain footballing landmarks. In January 2024, Darwin scored two goals in a 0-4 away win against Bournemouth. The first was his one hundredth career goal, and the second made him the first Premier League player to score ten goals and make ten assists in all competitions that season.

★ FOOTBALL RISING STARS ★

Standout goals included a volley from a ball that came over Darwin's shoulder as he ran into the box against West Ham, as well as a first-time hit shot from outside the area that curled into the bottom corner of the net against Burnley.

In a match against Brentford, the ball looped into the goal after Darwin chipped it over the standing goalkeeper. It would have been easier to go around the goalkeeper and shoot to the side, or simply square it to his teammate who was in so much space he might as well have been in outer space, but Darwin's interesting method showed his good form and growing confidence.

He'd already made a massive improvement since his first season. Darwin himself admitted he'd struggled in that first season with Liverpool, not helped by the language barrier he was starting to overcome.

Some problems remained, though. Despite the improvements in his game and overall stats, he drew criticism from some people for missing chances.

Once again, Darwin was about to prove any doubters

wrong. As the season continued, he had more goal involvements than players such as Kylian Mbappé and Robert Lewandowski!

In a game against Bournemouth in the League Cup (also known as the EFL Cup or Carabao Cup), the Bournemouth fans cheered after Darwin was unable to control a pass that took the ball away from him. But their joy was very short-lived.

Darwin immediately retrieved the ball, cut inside and curled it into the net from the

★ **DARWIN NÚÑEZ** ★

 corner of the penalty area. Somewhat deservedly, he taunted the Bournemouth fans by cupping his ear to them as he ran away to celebrate the goal.

Then a goal against Norwich in the FA Cup meant Darwin became the first player in Europe to reach double figures for non-penalty goals as well as assists.

Back in the League Cup, Darwin continued to help Liverpool progress. The team were 0-1 down in the first leg of the semi-final against Fulham, then Darwin came off the bench and assisted both goals in a 2-1 win. Liverpool drew 1-1 in the second leg to progress to the final.

Darwin missed the final through injury, but Liverpool beat Chelsea 1-0 after extra time.

Darwin also contributed five goals in the Europa League campaign, making him the second Uruguayan in the history of the competition to have over ten goal involvements (nine goals and two assists). Liverpool managed to make it to the quarter-final, but they were knocked out

DARWIN NÚÑEZ

of the competition by Italian club Atalanta.

As the 2023/2024 season came to an end, Liverpool, Manchester City and Arsenal were in a three-way fight for the Premier League title.

While Salah was out due to injury, Darwin carried the Liverpool attack, contributing important goals and assists. His eighteen goals and thirteen assists in all competitions put Liverpool in touching distance of more victories in Klopp's final season at the club. Unfortunately, the Premier League was not one of them, as Liverpool finished a respectable third.

Klopp got a heroic send-off at the end of the season, having made a huge impact on the fans and players throughout his time at the club. Whoever replaced him had a lot to live up to. Not just at the club, but also for Darwin.

In his time at Liverpool, Klopp had publicly been Darwin's biggest fan. He had supported and encouraged the footballer to improve his skills … and Darwin certainly had!

★ DARWIN NÚÑEZ ★

By the end of the 2023/2024 Premier League, Darwin had forty-six shots on target, hit the woodwork nine times and scored eleven goals. Whatever he did next was sure to be incredible.

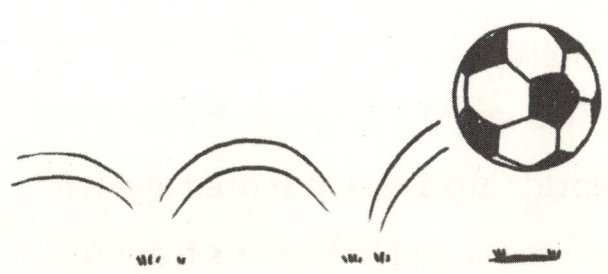

13
A QUALIFYING MACHINE

After making his full international debut, Darwin didn't make many appearances for his country due to injury.

In a qualifying game for the 2022 World Cup, Darwin scored against Columbia and helped his team to a

★ DARWIN NÚÑEZ ★

0-3 victory. His only other game was a 0-2 defeat to Brazil a few days later. He wouldn't play for Uruguay again for nearly a year.

During the 2021 Copa América, he was still out with injury. Uruguay certainly missed him, as they only scored four goals and lost on penalties to Columbia in the quarter-final.

Darwin also couldn't play in a few of the remaining World Cup qualification matches,

coming onto the pitch in five out of twelve games. He didn't score any goals or make any assists, but to be fair he was only in the starting eleven for two of those five games.

Thanks to a late run of four back-to-back wins, Uruguay were able to qualify. However, the 2022 World Cup itself was not a happy one for the country, as they failed to advance past the group stages on goal difference. Again, Darwin didn't score a goal in the tournament.

Not surprisingly, the Uruguayan media were critical of Darwin. In particular, they said it was bad how he had struggled against the thirty-

DARWIN NÚÑEZ

nine-year-old Portugal defender Pepe. These comments were echoed by other people across the world, including England's pundits – who were quick to criticise Darwin again. But this time, they may have had a point.

Going into the first round of matches for the 2026 World Cup qualifiers, Darwin had only scored a total of three goals and made zero assists in fourteen appearances for Uruguay. A big chunk of those games were while he was scoring goals for Benfica, so it may have been something of a surprise that he couldn't do the same for his country.

Some players just don't adjust well to international football, with the style or quality being just a little too much for them, and it looked like Darwin might be one of those players.

Despite many believing he didn't have it in him, Darwin defied his critics once more.

In the first 2026 World Cup qualifier against Chile, Darwin laid off a perfect short pass for Uruguay's first goal. Later in the game, he delivered a low cross across the

DARWIN NÚÑEZ

goal to set up an easy second goal.

He was very unlucky not to score himself, having two good chances. The first was a long-range effort that went over the bar, and the second was a cheeky drag back and shot that was well saved. Uruguay went on to win the game 3-1.

After Uruguay lost 2-1 to Ecuador, Darwin scored his first goal of the qualifiers in the next game against Columbia. Into injury time and losing 2-1, Uruguay won a penalty. Darwin didn't hesitate to place the ball on the spot and take the responsibility.

The goalkeeper guessed the right way, but the ball was too high for him to reach and flew into the top left corner of the net. Darwin had made it 2-2!

After three games, Uruguay had four points and faced the daunting task of playing both Brazil and Argentina in the next two games.

Uruguay came up against Brazil first. They played in front of over 52,000 fans in the Estadio Centenario in the capital Montevideo, where a young Darwin had moved to when he signed for Peñarol.

⭐ DARWIN NÚÑEZ ⭐

Darwin was the standout player. He scored the opening goal in the 42nd minute, with a standing header from ten yards out that beat the goalkeeper at the near post.

Later in the game, he received the ball from a throw-in on the byline. Immediately under pressure from two defenders, Darwin twisted and turned. Just as the ball was going out of play, he poked his foot out and knocked the ball back to a waiting player, who blasted the ball into the net. In a famous victory for Uruguay, the match ended 2-0.

Next up was the trip to face the reigning World Cup champions: Argentina.

Argentina were on a long winning streak, having won fourteen times in a row, but they failed to do anything with their early domination of the game against Uruguay.

Uruguay scored late into the first half and desperately held onto their lead. Argentina pushed for an equaliser, leaving themselves exposed to a counter-attack. And when a player is as quick

DARWIN NÚÑEZ

as Darwin, a dangerous counter-attack can quickly turn fatal.

A through ball just inside Uruguay's half sent Darwin clean through. Running the length of the half as a defender gave chase, Darwin dummied a shot before placing the ball past Emiliano Martínez in the Argentinian goal to make it 2-0. Yet again, Darwin's ability had helped Uruguay achieve another huge win.

Just a few days later, back on home soil in Montevideo, Darwin gave a Man of the Match performance, with two goals against Bolivia in a 3-0 win.

His first goal was a volley from a cutback pass, and the second was a header from close range.

In the first six games of the group, Darwin had scored five goals and made three assists, helping Uruguay reach second place and be in a great position going into the next batch of games in 2025.

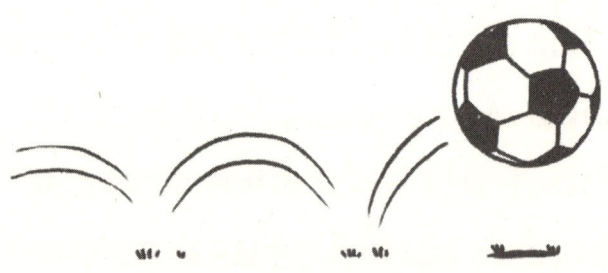

14
AGENT OF CHAOS

Darwin is one of the most divisive players currently in the modern game. Some fans think he's no good, while others think he's among the best players on the planet.

He is often labelled as an 'agent of chaos', a somewhat half compliment that means he can be unpredictable in his style of play.

The sad truth is that people rarely notice when a player does something good, unless they do it all the time. But when a player does something wrong, even if it's just once, many will start to complain and compare. Arguably, this is how people have viewed Darwin throughout his career so far. They point to his misses, but they themselves are missing everything he gets right.

Uruguay have had three world-class strikers in recent history: Edinson

DARWIN NÚÑEZ

Cavani, Luis Suárez and Diego Forlán. Between them, they have scored over 1,000 goals for club and country. Darwin has been compared to all three in his short career, said to have the individual strengths of each player: Cavani's speed and physicality, Suárez's skills and Forlán's finishing.

These skills add to the 'agent of chaos' label Darwin has been given. His unpredictable style can turn a game around and leave defenders helpless, letting Darwin get into dangerous positions.

Besides, being an 'agent of chaos'

isn't a bad label. If anything, it's actually very useful. If a player is unpredictable, if it seems that even they don't know what they're going to do next, then no opposition player will either. Embrace the chaos!

Darwin is seen to fail more simply because he tries harder. He is resilient in all situations, and his determination to overcome difficulties is unwavering. He won't stop or take no for an answer.

Darwin proved this in the 2024 Copa América, getting off to a great start by scoring in Uruguay's first group game against Panama.

★ DARWIN NÚÑEZ ★

He scored again against Bolivia, after running between two defenders to meet Maximiliano Araújo's pass. Having won every group game, Uruguay topped the table and made it through to the next round!

The quarter-final against Brazil was very tough. Darwin had a good chance to score via a close-range header in the 35th minute, but unfortunately he missed. The game ended 0-0 and went to penalties, which Uruguay won 4-2.

FOOTBALL RISING STARS

Uruguay went into the semi-final against Columbia positively, but it didn't go their way. Sadly, they lost 1-0.

Despite the loss, one good thing came out of the competition. Many Liverpool fans saw that Darwin's confidence had grown, giving them hope that he will perform well in the 2024/2025 season.

No matter how many goals Darwin scores or misses in the upcoming season, he is a player with limitless potential and a bright future.

Darwin is certainly a rising star playing the game in his own way.